WEASELS

WILD ANIMALS OF THE WOODS

Lynn M. Stone

The Rourke Press, Inc.
Vero Beach, Florida 32964

PHOTO CREDITS
© Breck Kent: title page; © Tom and Pat Leeson: pages 4, 8, 17,
21; © Tom Ulrich: cover, page 15; © Lynn M. Stone: pages 7, 10,
12, 13, 18

Library of Congress Cataloging-in-Publication Data

Stone, Lynn M.
    Weasels / Lynn Stone.
        p. cm. — (Wild Animals of the woods)
    Includes index.
    ISBN 1-57103-097-2
    1. Weasels—North America—Juvenile literature.
[1. Weasels.]   I. Title II. Series: Stone, Lynn M.   Wild Animals of
the woods.
QL737.C25S77 1995
599.74' 447—dc20   94–46894
                                                         CIP
                                                          AC

Printed in the USA

TABLE OF CONTENTS

WEASELS

Don't count the lean little weasel out in a fight. These long-bodied hunters attack animals much larger than themselves. Most weasels weigh just four or five ounces, but their quickness and fierceness make up for size.

Three **species** (SPEE sheez), or kinds, of weasels live in North America—the least, long-tailed and short-tailed, or ermine.

Each fall weasels in the the North undergo a change. Their brown summer coats turn white for winter.

A short-tailed weasel poses in its winter white coat

HOW THEY LOOK

Weasels' brown coats blend nicely with their summer surroundings. Except for black eyes and tail tips, they wear the perfect winter **camouflage** (KAM o flahj), too.

Weasels are so long and slender they almost look like a hot dog in fur. The long-tailed weasel from nose to tip of tail measures between 14 and 28 inches. The ermine measures nine to 17 inches. The least weasel is just seven-and-one-half to 10 inches long.

In summer camouflage, a weasel blends with its surroundings

WHERE THEY LIVE

Ermine and least weasels live throughout Alaska and Canada and in parts of the northern 48 states. The long-tailed weasel lives throughout the lower 48 states, except in the southwestern desert and on the Florida peninsula. It also lives in northern Mexico and southwestern Canada.

Weasels live in many different **habitats** (HAB uh tats), or special types of surroundings. Weasels are found on the **tundra** (TUN druh) of the Far North, in meadows and in dense forests.

A long-tailed weasel pauses from its hunt in a snowy field

HOW THEY ACT

Weasels are generally **nocturnal** (nahk TUR nul), but they don't limit their hunting to nighttime. In fact, summertime brings almost 24-hour daylight to weasels in the Far North.

Weasels have keen ears and a sharp sense of smell. They can slip swiftly into almost any hole or cranny. They can swim and climb trees.

Weasels are quite fearless. Long-tailed weasels have attacked people who have moved between them and their **prey** (PRAY).

A short-tailed weasel returns to daylight after prowling through an Arctic ground squirrel's burrow

Ground squirrels are a favorite prey of weasels

The American mink is a weasel-like animal of streamsides

PREDATOR AND PREY

Weasels are amazing **predators** (PRED uh tors). Predators kill other animals for food. With a bite to the back of the head, weasels regularly kill prey larger than themselves.

The least weasel kills mostly meadow mice, but its larger weasel cousins kill rabbits, ground squirrels, birds and other animals. A weasel can eat one-third of its body weight every day.

Weasels run quickly and follow the zig-zag path of their prey. The weasel's shape allows it to follow animals into burrows.

A short-tailed weasel kills its mouse prey with a bite to the back of its head

WEASEL BABIES

Baby weasels are usually born in April or May. A mother weasel may have as many as 18 babies, but six is average.

Baby weasels are born in a nest in a burrow. The mother lines the nest with bits of fur from animals she has killed.

Young weasels begin to hunt with their mother when they are about two months old. Weasels are nearly full grown at four months of age.

Young weasels grow quickly into adults

THE WEASEL'S COUSINS

Weasels are the smallest members of the group of meat-eating mammals called mustelids. Sea otters, sometimes weighing 80 pounds, are the largest mustelids.

Minks, martens, black-footed ferrets, badgers, fishers, skunks, wolverines and sea otters are also North American mustelids.

Martens, ferrets and minks look very much like weasels. Their coats do not change color, however, and they usually live in different habitats.

The pine marten, a close cousin of weasels, hunts through the tree tops

WEASELS AND PEOPLE

Many people think weasels are "bloodthirsty." They are probably no more "bloodthirsty" than any other hunting animal. Predators, including weasels, normally kill only what they can eat. If prey is easily within reach, however, many predators will kill more than they need. Chicken farmers, for example, may find that a weasel has killed several chickens during one hunt.

Weasels are generally useful to people, even farmers, because they kill large numbers of rats and mice.

Trappers catch ermine and long-tailed weasels for their white winter fur.

Trappers take weasels in winter for their rich, white fur

THE WEASEL'S FUTURE

Ermine and long-tailed weasels are fairly common. Least weasels are probably less common, but none of the weasels is in danger of disappearing.

Pine martens, which are "tree weasels," have suffered from too much trapping. Many states now protect martens. Some states are helping martens to make a comeback by releasing martens that have been caught in other areas.

Glossary

camouflage (KAM o flahj) — fur or feathers that match the color of an animal's surroundings

habitat (HAB uh tat) — the kind of place in which an animal lives, such as woodland

nocturnal (nahk TUR nul) — active at night

predator (PRED uh tor) — an animal that kills other animals for food

prey (PRAY) — an animal that is hunted by another for food

species (SPEE sheez) — within a group of closely related animals, one certain kind, such as a *long-tailed* weasel

tundra (TUN druh) — the low-lying, treeless plant cover of huge areas of the Far North

INDEX

7 3/98
9 8/99
15 10/00
24 9/04
31 4/09